Little Book
Big Testimony

Little Book
Big Testimony

*How Vulnerability
Led to Victory*

Josephine Joy Whyte

Charleston, SC
www.PalmettoPublishing.com

Little Book Big Testimony

First Edition

Paperback ISBN: 979-8-8229-2122-1
Hardcover ISBN: 979-8-8229-2121-4

Table of Contents

Introduction

Beginning with full transparency, I'd say the thought of writing this book scared me quite a bit. I always struggled with finding my voice; I'd describe it as my mind going a mile a minute when trying to articulate what I was thinking, yet the execution wasn't as flawless and profound as I would like. However, I'd always felt this freedom flow in writing, but thoughts of "Who are you to write a book?" began to surface.

Then I heard God whisper, "Just start." And so I did. The Holy Spirit, as usual, reminded me of men and women just like me who felt unqualified for their assignment, and through that I began to understand more and more that "God doesn't call the qualified, He qualifies the called." So with the strength of Almighty God, I began.

Now when I said I always struggled to find my voice, it may sound weird to people who had been there in different seasons of my life because I had always been vocal. I often felt like a popular loner; I would be surrounded by people but eagerly waiting for the relief I felt in being alone.

I'd also learned the difference between speaking from the place of my true voice and the one I think people wanted to hear. Since a child, I had always been a vulnerable soul, so vulnerable that, for a long time, I hated it about myself, until God began a work in me that revealed so much, and one of those was my vulnerability being a power that He had blessed me and so many others with.

I know society labels vulnerability as a weakness, something we should shy away from, but I want to encourage anyone who may be struggling with these false narratives to know that God's strength is made perfect in our weakness. So I pray you embrace your vulnerability and find power in your vulnerability because through it comes honesty, edification, and inspiration. Learning your voice all over again is an essential part of becoming; it is as a baby hearing their voice for the first time.

Throughout my life I've always felt this calling inside. I knew I was different and called for something far beyond my imagination. If you asked me ten years ago what I thought that feeling was, I would have told you it was me knowing I was destined to be a star—a star to the world—but glory be to God that what I was hearing was my calling to shine my light to the world so my Father, my Creator, *the One* who put the light within me, can be glorified. I thank and love Him so much for loving me enough to have that revealed to me.

As I was growing up, writing was my most comfortable form of expression—anything from notes to my friends to poetry and music—and now I believe the most significant was my testimony. My sister would always tell me that my life was one of many, and as the one living it out, I'd definitely agree with that. I knew I needed to share my testimony but wasn't sure how. I'd watched numerous testimonies on YouTube, becoming more and more inspired to share mine. I even tried picking up my phone and hitting record a few times, and every time I'd look, I'd be about an hour and a half in and nowhere close to being done.

Anyone who knew me knew just how much I enjoyed sharing every detail of a story, painting the picture for clarity, but that was me, understanding that the tiny details made all the difference. I kept organizing my thoughts, knowing that my testimony was something I needed to share with the world. After all, that was what *Jesus* wants us to do after receiving miracles so others may know the grace and mercy available to us through our heavenly Father.

I am blessed to say I have had many miracles from God in my life, as we all have whether we have noticed them or not, and it is my great privilege to share mine with you.

*"For assuredly, I say to you, whoever says to this mountain,
"Be removed and be cast into the sea, and does not doubt in
his heart, but believes that those things he says will be done,
he will have whatever he says."*

—MARK 11:23

Little Girl, Evil World

As a young girl, I'd always felt things deeply, possibly deeper than others, at least to my understanding. I grew up on a small block in South Jamaica, Queens, in a house with my parents and big brother. We were actually living in the hood at the time, but my home was so warm, and we felt so much love from my parents that I had no idea. I held on to a few sweet memories like my mom making pancakes with iced chocolate milk while my dad played Stevie Wonder, Marvin Gaye, the Temptations, Anita Baker, Bob Marley, Beres Hammond, and the list of soul music could go on. You name it, my dad played it!

My grandmother's house was around the corner; my aunt, a couple of uncles, and cousins all lived there. Looking back, I could never understand how my grandmother managed to cook, give love, and be everything to everyone. She was amazing, and I'd tell you more about her a little later.

Growing up with my cousins was a true blessing; we learned so much from one another.

Memories are truly something special.

To describe me as a little girl, I was what you would call a sweet handful—sassy, sensitive, cried when I didn't get my way. To be fair, I only behaved this way with my parents. God bless them. I was a daddy's girl, and I loved it there!

I would dance at almost every family event or work summer function my dad would take me to. My aunt would place bets on me winning like I was a trained dancer, although I was a trained ballerina for a bit. My dad would just put me in the center when music came on, and all I'd need to hear was, "Go, Jojo! Go, Jojo!" And I was on with the Bogle mixed with a few other classic Jamaican moves. Ha! But the Bogle was my go-to dance that I knew would steal the show. Good times!

Next day I'd be outside with my cousins playing two-hand touch football. My cousins, by the way, were all boys, with me being the only girl at the time. Oh, how the ratio tables had turned in my family these days! It was so interesting to see; my cousins and I would be outside, playing any chance we had. Children these days would never know that experience, those summer days. My grandmother would be outside the top window of the house, yelling for us to come inside before the sun set.

As I thought of my grandmother, I paused in awe of her beauty—absolute beauty. You know when you'd hear, "You might be the only Bible someone reads"? Well, the example of love my grandmother exemplified as the matriarch of our family was nothing short of divine. I stood in front of my grandmother as she got the news of my grandfather, her husband, being murdered by thieves while on his way to sending her a letter from Jamaica. Somehow she endured the pain while never stopping from loving us for one minute. She was and had always been the person to show me that love is more than gentle, compassionate, caring, and kind, but it can be all that wrapped up in fearless strength.

I always made myself the center of attention, just fearless! Man, you couldn't tell me I wasn't going to grow up and be either Brandy or Monica and forget that when Beyonce went solo, it was over. And we have the same birthday; that was it! LOL. I was her, and she was me, OK?

Thank God for wisdom in knowing what I know now. I don't desire to be anyone but who God has created me to be.

My brother and I were on the phone the other day, and he reminded me of a time my dad took us to an office BBQ one summer, and you couldn't tell me I wasn't Oprah, chile. LOL. I organized a group of business executives like it was second nature for me. This was before my light went out. Here was when things got dark, ladies and gentlemen, so brace yourselves because it's important that I begin by just saying it. Exposing the wound for surgery before the healing.

At the age of six or seven, I was sexually assaulted, raped multiple times, by a family friend; his name was Nakia. He and his sister spent a couple of summers with us, and little did I know one summer would change my life for the rest of my life.

My age at the time was always a blur to me; I only know it was during the time we lived in our childhood home, and I also know now that trauma can block out some details and highlight others. I often wonder, "Wow, God knew the traumas we'd have to go through in the world, and His design of us allows our bodies to process in bits and pieces, knowing reliving all at once can ruin us. What an awesome God!"

The first time it happened, everyone was right downstairs; he took me upstairs of *my* home, where he was staying for the summer; laid me down; placed a pillow over my face; and had sex with me laying there frozen like a doll, crying under the pillow. He did this almost every day that summer. The attic was a huge, dark space with a window at the left side of the room, across the way of the staircase. Upstairs was the place my family had parties for me when I was a baby among other family functions. So it went from a room of joy and now it was the room my innocence was ripped from my soul. He was a teenager, and again, I was maybe six or seven years old.

I didn't tell my parents or anyone for a long time. I buried my pain into the deepest, darkest place of my soul that slowly started to surface. Remember when I expressed writing being my most comfortable form of expression? Well, my diary was the only thing that knew of the abuse:

If the pages could talk, it'll tell you of my darkest moments buried in the depths of my soul. If the pages could talk, it'll tell you of pain that feels new when I know it's old; it's an ugly, evil trick, and I know it. I need to become the best version of myself, and I won't let this feeling blow it, blow it for me, blow it for the vision I see, that God has implanted, and I know that he waters. Though I am broken, I will be put back together, even more beautiful, by the One who knows all and is willing and able—my heavenly Father.

I began to become more and more exposed to the toxicity happening all around me. My family had been functioning in a vicious cycle of physical and mental abuse for generations, and the worst part about it was that as time went by, the more normalized it became.

I remember the summer days where it'll quickly go from playing outside my aunt's house with my cousins to jumping on my uncle's back, using all my strength to stop him from beating her. I remember running back outside after coming in from playing to the same uncle exposing himself to me while walking out of the bathroom from a shower. I remember going from being beaten with an cord of an iron to staying up late, singing while my brother played guitar until I was able to fall asleep. I remember hearing stories of my uncle shooting my aunt in the leg after they got into a fight and us laughing it off many years later under the guise of "Our family is crazy, man."

Whenever there'd be a celebration, in the moment of a good time, I'd step back and look at the potential of our strong, beautiful, and powerful family. I would feel and still feel this sense of happiness and an overwhelming feeling of sadness all at the same time. I felt sadness knowing the foundation had never been solid. I saw the years of operating in dysfunction, oblivious to the trickling effects it had had generationally. We were blind to the chains we'd learned to function in instead of doing the work to break free from them. Nonetheless, deep down everyone knew it was there, but no one acknowledged it because, in acknowledging it, we'd have to confront it, and no one had the tools to mend or fix the broken foundation that had been in place longer than anyone could remember.

So, we hurt one another; we let others hurt us, not understanding why, or we hurt in silence. Along my journey, I had to make a conscious decision to step away and allow Jesus to heal me in order for my family to have a fighting chance. I thank God for the privilege of knowing that he is truly the only way out of bondage of any kind.

Statistics show that being a victim of sexual abuse makes you susceptible to more abuse. While I choose not to follow statistics of society but only the true living word of my God, that tells me I am healed through the stripes of Jesus Christ. I do, however, know that when going through something as dark and evil as sexual abuse, the healing is an arduous journey. It can rip away at your identity, which is why the enemy tries to attack from such a young age; it is sickening.

Your self-worth can become defined by the abuse. I understand because I have experienced different forms of abuse that I can find freedom in sharing to help anyone who has buried it far away or may not even know how to identify it, but your body does to the point you can live consumed by that same fear from the moment it has taken place.

There was this older man who lived on the block I grew up on who told a lie that I was "into him". I might have been thirteen or fourteen at the time, if not younger. I never said anything to him other than a cordial hello or goodbye out of respect. I was a teenage girl simply living her life, oblivious of more predators I'd need to look out for. I found out this rumor from my aunt who had had a few drinks and actually said it to me as if it was funny. Funny? After hearing this, I was just sitting there, body frozen and full of rage at the same time. It brought me right back to that sexual abuse, like a scab being aggressively gnawed at.

The thing was no one ever addressed it, not even me. I just never spoke a word to him ever again after that, not to mention I'd still have to see him around from time to time. I was just hoping an adult would step in and come to my rescue to call him out for the liar he was. There I was, taking on a shame that didn't even belong to me, unprotected and afraid to speak up for myself, drowning out my voice even more.

Oftentimes we, as young women or men, experience traumatic events that start to affect our body like a disease if we bury and don't acknowledge them. We bury them because everyone else does, making us feel crazy.

I know it eats at you like a parasite that gets bigger with every abuse, every rejection, every feeling of unworthiness, and every mistake. I want everyone reading this who has been a victim of abuse to locate that parasite,

X-ray it by speaking facts about that parasite, then *remove it*! Because *you* have the power to! *Do not let it eat away at your beautiful soul.*

Looking back, I saw my abuse as this poison that entered my body that slowly started to seep into other areas of my soul the older I got. The thing is when you bury pain so deep, by the time the pain from the trauma shows up, it is a lot to unpack all at once.

It isn't until now that I wonder, "If I were that same little girl, use to getting all the attention to my detriment as I grew older, would I be as compassionate? Would I be as sensitive and empathetic to others' pain as I am now had this not happened to me?" See? Sometimes God needs to break our hearts for it to be unhardened, and other times—times like these—our broken heart draws him nearer and leads to our deliverance.

So what the enemy meant for evil, our heavenly Father uses to produce good. So never let the enemy take your joy in the midst of a trial. Look at your joy as your secret weapon; even when you can't see the physical battle being won by keeping your joy, you are more than a conqueror in the spiritual realm, the everlasting realm.

"Would I be as sensitive to God's voice today without my pain?" "The Lord is close to the brokenhearted and saves those who are crushed in spirit" (Psalm 147:3, NIV). This scripture lets me know God is there with me. I know we often wonder, "Why do bad things happen to us?" My answer to that is read the Bible. Look around; wake up! We live in an evil world, which is why God tells us not to be of this world (Romans 12:2).

I look at it like this: when you go through a trial with someone, you grow closer. You know that saying "Lemme know it's real"? God is going to take what the enemy meant for evil and use it for your good. Now I may not have quite figured out the purpose of this particular trial yet in life, but *even if that means me seeking and growing God in spite of.* I can't think of a better "in yo' face" to the enemy than that, and I'm good with that. Hey, you know, I think I just found its purpose right in this moment with you. *I will praise him in all ways always through it all.*

As I grew older and began to heal, I would tell myself my abuser was also a child himself, and maybe this also happened to him; who knows? But what I do know is I carried that hate for him over to my parents and myself, and it wasn't until seven years ago that I'd learned to let go of this hate completely, and I'll explain how. Before I do, I want to get really transparent about my pain and my experience through this pain.

My parents got divorced a year after I was sexually assaulted; my world just felt like a tornado—a tornado I was going through alone. Of course, I am aware my elder brother was going through this with me, but when you're going through something like sexual abuse, you feel a different type of isolation. I felt as if I was on an island by myself—at least an island is beautiful, so let's just say I felt like I was screaming at the top of my lungs, but no one heard me; life was just doing what it did. I was watching everything being taken up in chaos in the air, revolving around me. It was rough, an emotional disaster.

Now I sit here and wonder, "What if I told my parents what happened to me? Would they have stayed together?" For a while, I'd feel a strong conviction of answering that question with a yes. I do believe and know there is power in truth, and the Word of God tells us there is life and death in the power of the tongue. I know more than I did then that my parents loved me very much and would have done what was needed to protect me, which I believe would have taken precedent over their issues at the time, put things into perspective, so to speak. Maybe. What do I know about what was supposed to be? I leave that to the One who is running things.

I want to take a moment and tell any girl or woman with that inner little girl who is still healing and reading this right now. I want to tell you something I wish someone told me then if they knew. *God sees you, God loves you, and God is with you in the darkest time and is carrying you through. He will never leave you nor forsake you. He makes all things work together for those who love him. In this world we will face trials, but be of good cheer; Christ has overcome the world* (John 16:33). *And that same Christ lives in us. We won't understand the hard times in the moment, but trust God through it and know he's making a way and sees all.*

Also, tell someone, preferably right away; but if not right away, I don't care if it is twenty years later. Just tell someone. The more you speak about it, the more you're set free from the bondage it holds on your soul. You may ask, "So why did God allow this happen to me?" If you would have asked me this at ten, fifteen, eighteen, or twenty-five years old, I wouldn't be able to answer that for you because I needed the answer myself.

I know the next thing I'm going to say may sound discouraging, but it wasn't until I went through more darkness that I was able to see that all my pain had purpose. Just like before we were born into this world, in the womb, we were taught we must go through the darkness before we got to the light. Once I learned that, I then became grateful for every tear and every ache because in that I became dependent on *my Lord and Savior*. God's strength was made perfect in my weakness.

I learned that I don't need to figure it out on my own, and by knowing *him* and *only* through knowing him was I able to truly know who I was and am, my worth. Heir of the Most High—that's who you are, and no mortal being on this planet can take that away from you. Your only job is to remember and never forget!

When God created us, all was "very good." We were never meant to know evil, and to be clear, there is a huge distinction between knowing something and personally knowing it. So again, I remind you *we were never meant to know evil.*

You see, my loves, we are born in a world full of darkness, and God tells us in his Word, "I have told you these things, so that in me you may have peace. In this world you will have trouble. But take heart! I have overcome the world" (John 16:33, NIV).

Like most Christians, when we think of trials, it causes us to reflect on Job. God's Word tells us that after Job faced many trials in this world caused by the enemy,

"Job sinned not, nor charged God foolishly." God knew this before ordaining the trial sent by satan because He knew the soul of Job.

As children of God, let us face every trial knowing that God trusts us enough to know we will rely on His strength, trusting Him, knowing that though it may seem difficult, our Father will turn it around for our good. Remind the enemy he has no power because trust that he knows it! He's just banking on us not knowing.

If only I knew then what I know now. After my parents divorced, my father moved uptown in the Bronx with his mother and other family—you know, "that side" of the family. My father's mother was one of those women who showed little to no emotion. I was hugged by her once in my entire life.

My mother, brother, and I moved to Rosedale into an apartment upstairs from my grandmother and across the street from one of my best friends—more divine hugs from God and his intentional, loving provision over my life. Little did I know that in this house I would go through some of the darkest times that would continue to shape my childhood, ultimately shaping me as a woman.

I began to see a side of my mother I never met before. She projected so much of her pain onto me that it was overbearing. I was a bit dithered over whether I should go into further detail about my experience of my mother. Reason being, I want to make sure I honor her while still honoring myself. The more I've lived, learned and experienced, the more I identify that we are multifaceted beings and that we all go through many different stages in our lives, most of which we aren't prepared for, and the more spiritual warfare becomes more apparent through the lenses of my spiritual eyes.

I began to pinpoint that a major attack from the enemy was that on the family and the effects that it then has on the family. For my mother, she was forced to be two different women. Before the divorce she was a happy wife and a mother, and then life happened, and she was now a single mother of two, working as a full-time registered nurse, not to mention having her own personal traumas that she never healed from.

Now does this mean this justifies a mother projecting her pain onto her children? No, of course not, but as I grew older, I learned grace and the importance of giving it to others who hurt you, especially a parent. You have to ask yourself, "Did they have the tools needed to heal?" You start imagining your trauma and think about theirs as a child and ask, "Who was there for them when they needed someone?" Although it taught me a lot about how to not be with my children, I also knew to never say what I would or wouldn't do until I walked in someone's shoes. So you see, we need to give one another grace to forgive, and we need to forgive to heal, and we need to heal to step into whom God has created us to be.

My brother was really my guardian angel growing up, especially during these formative years of my life. He has always had this incredibly calm, soothing spirit; it was truly amazing. Nothing really ever bothered him. To have this discipline from such a young age was nothing short of divine. Whenever I was sad, crying, or in so much pain that I couldn't sleep, my brother would get his acoustic guitar, and he'd play; I'd sing until I felt better.

As I looked back, my mother really struggled with a lot of suppressed pain, and I'm so grateful to God for creating my brother and having him be such a blessing in my life. My dad would come and pick us up every weekend. My brother and I eagerly looked forward to those weekends. Every week felt like I was holding breath until the exhale of relief I'd have when I saw my dad.

I believe both my parents felt they would make their way back to each other even after the divorce. It's mind blowing how quickly love can turn to hate.

Albert Einstein once said, "Energy cannot be created or destroyed; it can only be changed from one form to another." When two people who love each other deeply begin to fall out of love, I think there's no other evidence of this statement being true. In my mother's vulnerability, she was looking for healing in all the wrong places. I know now that when you haven't cultivated a relationship with God, not knowing He is with you, it will be hard to navigate through your pain, feeling alone.

Like most people, she tried to find her healing in a romantic relationship, which I think started out as receiving attention that she felt she didn't get from my father at the latter part of their marriage. Through that relationship I was blessed with my baby sister, Rachel. Ah, were we in love! The night my mother went into labor at the same hospital she worked, she was surrounded by so much love, and my brother and I were outside in the car, eagerly waiting for the phone call.

Seeing my sister for the first time was an experience; although she looked like an alien, she was the most adorable alien I'd ever seen, and I couldn't wait to begin this journey of being a big sister to her. So there I was, nine years older than my sister, ready to protect her from everything.

At around age eleven, my mother found religion; yes, I said religion, not *God*. Don't get it twisted, though, because religion led my mom to truly know God. Shortly after, we became Seventh-day Adventists, and my mother became extremely strict even more than she already was.

It threw me off a bit because, as I grew older, my mother struggled a bit with fighting off some demons that still dwelled in her inner little girl, and I seemed to be her punching bag. So our relationship weathered some real storms, which caused me to rebel against everything she tried to instill. See, in my eyes I looked at it like, "Girl, get your life together and stop taking your pain out on me before you try to tell me anything," a.k.a. what Jamaicans would call *outta audah*.

In reality my mother was trying to work through all her pain, hurt, loss, challenges, and heartache she'd faced. She carried so much pain without ever talking about it because that wasn't a thing in her generation. Also, keep in my mind that my mother is Carib from Kingston, Jamaica, born and raised, so talking about pain is seen as taboo.

My mother was and is an extremely talented seamstress, designer, and wife, not to mention the best cook you'd ever meet in your life! My mother can make anything taste good; it's truly amazing. She and my grandmother moved to the United States from Jamaica when my mother was in her early twenties. Here she worked hard to not only bring her six siblings up from Jamaica but also become a registered nurse while raising my brother and eventually me as well.

I looked back and thought about the knowledge my mother acquired while growing in her relationship with the Lord. It was like she was a child, and I meant that in the best way possible. The way she absorbed and retained information was beyond impressive and a blessing.

I looked at her life, and I thought about all her knowledge, and in that knowledge, it still didn't reveal her identity to her. You see, I'm learning the difference between knowledge and wisdom. Our older generation, though, had the knowledge and, I believe, often lacked an intimate relationship with God, therefore lacking the wisdom about what it is to be a part of the body of God and the understanding of what that truly means.

Us becoming Seventh-day Adventists, though, didn't truly make me understand the blessing of knowing the true Sabbath at the time. It had filled my life with so many blessings. I met my best friend in church. I went to all Adventist private schools for both junior high and high school, which not only brought some amazing people into myself but, I believe, had protected me as well.

As a young teen, I struggled with my self-worth a lot, constantly doubting myself, others, and I dare say God, not his existence but my existence in his eyes. I had questions like "God, do you see me?" Now I know not only has he never taken his eyes off me but he's also been with me and is always with me.

Unfortunately, not seeing that then allowed my sight to be set on everything else. My mother met an older man from the church we attended who was a part of church but apart from the church. Let me elaborate on what I meant exactly.

He was a part of a small organized group of Seventh-day Adventists who called themselves Davidians. They, as most Seventh-day Adventists, believe in the Sabbath day being the seventh day of the week (Saturday); they both believe in the spirit of prophecy. Now in the book of Revelation, God's Word tells us there will be a number of 144,000 that will receive the seal of God. "And I heard the number of the sealed, 144,000, sealed from every tribe of the sons of Israel" (Revelation 7:4, ESV). Davidians believe they are a part of that number and currently reside in the countryside, doing the Lord's work.

This man whom my mother began dating was a leader within this organization. Though he claimed himself to be a man of God, I felt extremely uncomfortable around him. One, he was still married at the time he began to pursue my mother; some may say my mother was to blame as well, and I could not totally disagree. I would say this though: there are predators who will sniff you out day and night until they find the right time to pounce. That was exactly what he did to my mother, and I had front row seats.

It wasn't long before she moved him in with us. He was completely inappropriate at times; he'd pull me to sit on his lap and comment on my looks, which would give me the creeps. I knew I'd never be subject to someone's perversion ever again in my life. So I gave my mother an ultimatum, all while telling my father to be prepared to come and get me. For a while my father would let me know he wasn't in the position to do so, so I had to sit tight and wait for when that time came. During that time, I struggled a lot with depression.

While I didn't understand the entirety of the situation while in motion, the weight of the change was prominent. As a child, all I knew was the change in the little things, the details—how my mornings went from the smell of warm pancakes and chocolate milk to having to figure it out on my own. Now as a grown woman reflecting, I understand the need for individual wholeness and God's design in that, the need for marriage, the necessity of a safe space of gentle thoughtfulness in love and protection for a woman, and the need of acceptance, gentleness, and safe space for a man for both to function at full capacity. If you ever listen to a woman or a man ready to grow their family, you often hear, "We just have so much love to give," almost like an overflow. Well, I believe that's the cup we should all be pouring from before bringing children into this world because of the effects of the lack of substance in said cup.

As parents we have to be extremely intentional about managing our emotions around our children because though they may not see everything, they feel everything, and those feelings stick if not dealt with. Now that I am blessed with my two beautiful children, I use my past experiences as a tool to be intentional about the mother I am and strive to be to my children. As a young person, most people don't understand just how difficult it is to be in a spiritual warfare unknowingly at such a young age. That is why it is so important that we are there to give our young people knowledge of the truth and love so they may know they have a heavenly Father who is fighting for them always and that they do not need go through this life carrying their feelings alone.

Thank God He had the escape ready while I was complaining because, in my sophomore year of high school, my daddy came to the rescue. So there I was, on my way to a new chapter from Queens to the suburbs of Yonkers, New York.

Around this time, I started to take music very seriously. I started working at the age of fourteen at a local sneaker store while in school and investing into my music at about age seventeen. Becoming a famous recording artist was my dream for many years. I wanted it so bad and felt like because I could sing, rap, and write, this was how it was supposed to look, and measuring up to society's standards, it was only natural to perceive it as such. The thing was, deep down, I felt like a fraud. I would put all these lyrics in my songs that painted the picture of me being something I wasn't, maybe something I wanted to be at the time but still wasn't.

I often look back and say now that if God created me and loves me, how did I really expect him to bless a fraud version of myself? I began to learn about myself a little more and grow. He'd revealed in many ways that that path couldn't have possibly been for me to evolve into who I was created to be. God warned us to "get out of her, my people" (Revelation 18:4, NWT), referring to Babylon, and I would have been right there, following my straight path to hell. I always knew how gentle natured and sensitive I was and that industry would have swallowed me whole, and my Father knew it.

The Light in the Dark

When I got pregnant with my son at twenty-three, it was such a beautiful and dark time because while I felt this immediate calm over me ,the minute that stripe turned to two. I just knew this little baby would flip my world upside down in the best way possible, and that he did. I never told anyone this, but I used to pretend to be pregnant when I was alone just to feel that feeling of being mommy, not knowing how much I truly wanted to be one. I used to be a bit apprehensive about sharing this part of my journey, but that's the thing I love about the truth: it's so real and vulnerable that even when it is far from perfect, it's somehow still so pure.

So let's rewind a bit and get into it. In high school, I had a friend who started off as a really good friend; I would call him my brother for many years, even played matchmaker for him and another girl in our school. Though we were both aware of each other being attractive, we never acted or even communicated about it, but we both knew the time and space wasn't right. We were both in relationships and honestly just weren't on either of our radars to explore more.

Over the years, time went by; we both graduated, remaining friends throughout. During this time, things began to slowly escalate into something more at around age eighteen or nineteen. We began to spend time together, and before we knew it, we began to explore our attraction and started hooking up occasionally, but we never really took each other seriously. We just thought we'd be those friends who'd end up together when the music chairs stopped, and it was just us two left.

Young ladies, please take this as a lesson in life. You are more precious than you can imagine but just as much as you can imagine. Think bigger! God calls you sacred because you are beautiful; accept nothing less than divine love. Some things that seem desirable and pleasurable are temporary feelings and permanent lies from the enemy to defile and steal your joy.

While in college, I met and began dating someone. We met in African American Studies. One day while in class, he tapped me on the shoulder, asking me for my notes' next thing I knew, we were inseparable. It was something out of a movie! We dated for three years, although it wasn't love looking from a hindsight perspective; the infatuation was so captivating that it felt like the closest imitation of it. We loved being around each other, and we had so much fun together; he called us two peas in a pod, and we were. Too bad I'd come to find out I wasn't the only pea in his pod.

Before I go into how much he hurt me, I want to share the ways he blessed me. When we first started dating, I felt free, conversations were deep, and he was really a beautiful and rare soul from an amazing family, doing the best with what life served him with, but he wasn't the one for me.

I knew for certain when, one weekend, he went away with his boys to Miami on Valentine's Day, Grammy weekend, and I couldn't get in touch with him. I already knew what time it was, not to mention the knowing in my gut of him cheating. That same night on Valentine's Day, while I sat there crying, feeling sorry for myself and, quite frankly, stupid, a text then came through, and guess who it was. No, I know what you're thinking. The person I'd been dating for three years? Well, no, not him. He was in a truly carefree, no-efs-given, man-child mode.

It was my close friend from high school whom I had been off and on with for years, asking if I wanted to link and catch up. It had also been a while since we saw each other, so the idea of catching up and seeing him was comforting and just what I needed.

So I cleaned my face off, jumped in the shower, and got myself ready to get picked up and get my mind off all the things my imagination was doing to my emotions. We went out that evening, caught up, and spent the night together; in the moment it felt like just want I needed. See, ladies, this is what I mean by temporary feelings producing permanent lies. Here I was, hurting because the man I was dating wasn't treating me less than I deserved, so I went and hooked up with a man who wasn't committed to me but justifying it with "he's my long-term friend whom I love" and "it's a sign." *No, no, no!* My uncertainty and worthiness were the signs that I drove right past.

Although I wanted to be with the man I was seeing for three years who I knew didn't deserve me, seeing my old friend just brought up more feelings I didn't have room to work through. So I ended up just throwing myself more into work and speaking to both occasionally while keeping my distance as I sorted out what I was feeling. It was one of the many experiences in my life where I'd learned I should trust God to work it out. It would turn out that time to myself was exactly what I needed. A couple of weeks went by, and I started to feel off, like something with my body was different from the norm.

A few weeks later while at work, I decided to take a pregnancy test because I hadn't been feeling like myself for a while. I remember the day perfectly; it was a beautiful day out. I casually went for a walk to the drugstore on my break at work and bought a test to take. I planned on waiting until I got home, but who was I kidding? I marched right in that bathroom and got to preparing.

I came to find out I was pregnant! I felt an immediate calm over my body like I just knew this baby inside of me was special. Now I'm sure most mothers feel that, but I just knew my child was going to make a difference in this world, and that was before I even met him. It was so bizarre, but it was nothing short of the truth.

Around the time I found out I was pregnant, my best friend and I were going through a very difficult time in our friendship. I'd always envisioned this moment with her by my side every step of the way, but life had other plans. Here I was, going through this life-changing chapter and overall not looking like anything I imagined it to be in so many ways. I had so many internal battles during my pregnancy; one of those battles was me thinking about the man I'd be raising my child with, highly aware it worked the other way around, but there I was, twenty-three, pregnant with my baby boy, and alone.

One day out of nowhere, I thought of my friend from high school possibly being the father but said, "There's no way. It was one time, and I'd been seeing my boyfriend for three years off and on." So I didn't entertain the idea for too long. I even prayed for it not to be. Man, the things I'd asked God for were so wild looking back. My perception was so clouded by lack that it led me to taking the man-child back.

In true man-child fashion, it was "all good" until finding out I was pregnant. As I looked back, it was amazing how many times God had warned me that this wasn't the man for me, even put the knowledge of the other women in me. Women, we always know that feeling we often call intuition; I call it the Holy Spirit constantly guiding. He let me know a few times before, but I ignored it because I couldn't see past what I thought I wanted.

It wasn't until I was around five months pregnant when I actually would catch him cheating, and it would be confirmed. How did I catch him? I went through his phone. I know, typical, but I sat there before opening that phone already knowing what I'd find but just thinking, "Is this what we've come to, Jo?" Up until then, I'd never gone through a man's phone, never cared to. Nonetheless, lo and behold, there it was, the inappropriate text from a girl at two in the morning. That was the beginning of another layer of internal battle I'd have to go through.

During my pregnancy, he would constantly remind me that this wasn't what he wanted. It wasn't the right time as if it was ideal for me. Any woman who has been through this knows what hearing that from someone whom you'll be raising a child with and whom you think you love feels like, how gut wrenching it is.

Now I'm not going to completely throw him under the bus; we were young, with him being a little younger than me, still finding his way. His parents were amazing, beautiful people both in and out, but after a while, his parents were stepping up more than him, and his best wasn't good enough for me, and I was and still am giving him grace because the truth is he was not giving his best. We were talking about the most precious, most important gift who depended on me for his happiness. I knew something had to change and fast.

So needless to say, my pregnancy was tough! I was sad a lot of the time, although I was also so excited about meeting my baby boy. I also think being especially careful about what I ate definitely played a huge role in how I felt mentally and emotionally, but it was *hard*.

God provided me with an amazing support team; my mother, sister and big brother. They always made sure I ate nutritious meals and were there to listen to me when I needed someone. I also worked throughout my pregnancy and was surrounded by the most amazing people I could have asked for during that time in my life; they truly felt like family. Since I worked up until I couldn't anymore, it was a welcomed distraction.

This brings me to the best morning of my life—the morning God blessed me with my baby boy. The evening before I got to the hospital, as any new mother, I felt all the things—nervous, happy, curious, overwhelmed, and overjoyed all in one. My baby boy wasn't quite ready to come that night, though, so I attempted to get some rest so that I was ready when he was.

That next morning, God revealed my first vision. I was lying in the hospital bed and woke up at what looked to be about five in the morning. I could see the reflection of the sun rising on the side of the building; everything was extremely quiet, so quiet that I knew I had to be dreaming, but honestly I was not too sure I was. I felt very much present. I looked over to my mother, who was fast asleep on that hospital chair (y'all know that chair I'm talking about), wrapped in the coziest blanket, resting so peacefully.

As I looked, I saw two men whom I would describe as giants, beautiful, brown skinned with curly, textured hair; they were walking around as if they were looking for someone. It didn't take long for them to stop at the window of our room, standing on opposite sides of the window. They looked at each other and then into the room.

I was so consumed by their presence that I can only imagine if they were looking directly at me, but they weren't. They looked in the room at me, in my direction but not directly; no words were spoken, but they had a look of satisfaction on both their faces as if they found whom they were looking for. It wasn't until I woke up that I realized they were looking for my unborn baby. I honestly still don't know if they were my angels or my sons.

That afternoon at 12:59 p.m., Nasallah was born (Nas from Nasir meaning "king" and Sallah meaning "good-spirited king," and that he was). My good-spirited young king came in at 7"11. I was completely in love with this little human who would one day call me Mommy. Being his mommy became the joy of my life; it came so naturally.

When he was about four months, I was presented with a job opportunity to relocate to California. I took some time to consider the opportunity, but in actuality it came at a perfect time as everything in God's timing. I didn't even know why I needed to be in California, but God knew.

Not even a month of being in California, I received news that would change my world forever. I wrestled with sharing this part of my testimony for the privacy and protection of my son. Let's just say I received the answer to my prayer where I mentioned the crazy things we asked God for. And it wasn't what I initially wanted it to be, but God knew what my son and I needed because it was for the better!

I couldn't see it then, but it was one of the biggest blessings of my life. My son has an amazing father, he always puts our son before himself, and I trust him to come through for mine always. Praise God for his Word. "All things work together for good to those who love God, to those who are called according to His purpose" (Romans 8:28, NKJV).

One thing about me was I prayed, not as often as I wished I did, but whenever I felt it in my soul that I needed to, I did.

God's grace and mercy is superb and overwhelming; my spirit cries in glory when I really sit back and think of the favor over my life. All glory to the Most High, the King of kings, my Provider, who knew me before I was in my mother's womb.

Two angels stood at my window to visit you just before your birth.

From the moment I held you, I knew this wasn't the first—the first time you existed, with a calm so beautiful that it shifted everything in my world.

How could this be that God loved me enough to give me you, so much so that he would have you look at me like you felt the same way too? Oh what gift!

Praise the Most High for knowing what I need to heal and break my heart all at once. This little human, 7.11 lb. with the cutest sounds, opened up my mind past space and time. God, I know he's yours first, but I love the feeling that he's also all mine.

Pillow of Prayer

Becoming a mother, though the most amazing blessing of my life, felt familiar in every way, as well as terrifying. As in love with my baby boy as I was, I also would have these waves of emotions that would flood in, this fear of my past trauma affecting this perfect, beautiful little life. There were so many times during my pregnancy that I would cry out to God for things to change or work in my favor, and the only thing I'd always say when I looked back at those prayers was, "Thank you, God, that your ways are higher than my ways and your thoughts are higher than my thoughts." Though the journey was hard, humiliating, and extricating, it turned out so beautiful! You know when people say, "I would do it all over again to get to this point"? Yeah, I wouldn't, but *I do thank and praise God* for teaching me the lessons I've learned through that pain, growing me, revealing me, and loving me through that pain and most importantly going through it with me.

I'd always felt *His* presence even when I forgot to pray; He was there. He sent me angels to watch over me. He gave me strength when I was exhausted from crying. He gave me peace when I was flooded with anxiety. What a *mighty God*! I get emotional every time I think of *the One*!

I almost titled this chapter "Don't Sleep on the Power of Prayer" because I did for so long. I wanted to start with the warning straight out the gate. I say warning because it is truly dangerous to live a life without praying to the One who is life.

Growing up, I would hear of the power of the prayer, but it wasn't until very recently that I truly understood and knew just how powerful. My mother and grandmother would always remind us to pray, and because of that reminder, I would feel the weight it carried in my spirit. I was continually learning. I would always pray those prayers of thanksgiving for my meals and at times before I'd go to sleep at night—y'all know that "Now I lay me down to sleep" prayer—until I began to experience this shift.

The Holy Spirit was revealing to me that prayer was more than I could even imagine, and if I wanted to truly hear from God the way I was seeking to hear from God, I'd need to become more comfortable speaking to *him*. You never want to be that friend you only hear from when you need something. You want to be present through the ups and downs, you want that person to know you can be trusted, and you want to be there when needed so when and if you ever need anything, you'll feel more comfortable because you know the relationship is give-and-take.

Now let's imagine the beautiful, unfailing love of God, who needs nothing from us but a willing heart. God has created us with the freedom of choice because what is true love without liberty?

I would have these waves of sadness; I knew I was blessed, and I needed nothing. Now were there things I wanted to make my life more comfortable? Most certainly, but I knew my heavenly Father knew it before I did and was again working it all out for my good. Knowing all that still did not change how I'd feel from time to time, and I honestly felt like I was going crazy.

Well, one night while venting to one of my best friends, she then reminded me to pray. Now it was not like this was something out of the ordinary; my girls and I would speak of prayer often. Whenever you find yourself venting to people more than usual, this is a clear sign that more prayer is required for God to fix the very thing you're venting about. I'll be the first to tell you that expressing yourself is completely normal and healthy because it is. Just always remember to give it to God first; talk to God first.

The Bible tells us so much about prayer that I can witness to. "But when you pray, go into your room, close the door and pray to your Father, who is unseen. Then your Father, who sees what is done in secret, will reward you" (Matthew 6:6, NIV).

"Do not be anxious about anything, but in every situation, by prayer and petition, with thanksgiving, present your requests to God" (Philippians 4:6, NIV).

Oh! And one of my favorites is Romans 8:26 (NIV). "In the same way, the Spirit helps us in our weakness. We do not know what we ought to pray for, but the Spirit himself intercedes for us through wordless groans." When you go through things with God, you learn what to pray for, to sometimes just sit there with Him in silence, and to cry out to him.

There's so much beauty when you really sit and think about the true intimacy in prayer. Just imagine two scenarios. First, imagine you've received good news and can't wait to share it with your best friend, so you tell him or her to come over so you all can catch up and celebrate together. Second, think of when you come into a trial, you need that best friend to come over so you can cry and vent whatever you need to help make that pain go away for a little bit. Now though I'm unable to speak anyone else's experience, you find that it helps.

Now paint the picture of you praying to *the One* who sees and knows all, who can help change your situation, and who can reveal the purpose of said trial to you. Facing hard times can be extremely difficult, lonely, and consuming, and you want to know who knows that? Your adversary. The Bible tells us the enemy waits like a roaring lion to see whom he may destroy. So of course, as the coward he is and as the father of lies, he makes you think your pain is more than your life itself. My brothers and sisters, please be encouraged that God has a plan for your life. Jesus has died for that plan, so it is in our best interest to *live for that plan*, and to get to that plan, we will face seasons of long-suffering, but the reward will reveal the purpose for it.

From East to West

Living in California was a complete life-changing experience for me. The Word of God says, "Consider it pure joy...whenever you face trials" (James, 1:2, NIV). And, baby, living three thousand miles away from everything and everyone I'd ever known as a new single mother was definitely a trial. Mind you, before living in California, I'd visited a few times, and you couldn't tell me this wasn't where I'd end up living until I actually lived there. The thing was it wasn't so much about the place as it was the timing, and in retrospect although I was depressed while living there, God knew it was where I needed to be to go through that trial in that particular season, not to mention the angel He blessed me with and worked through.

Her name was Roxy. I tell you, this girl was sent from God. I say this because there was no other possible explanation. This young woman who did not know me, out of the kindness of her heart, was there for me and my son every step of the way. I honestly probably should have named this chapter about my experience in California

"Roxy, the angel." She would pick my son and I up every morning for work and drop me after; some days she would let me run errands in her car.

Some mornings when I wasn't working (which was rare), I would take my son on long car rides out to Malibu, and I tell you, those long car rides and trips to see the ocean and sunset healed my soul a little more each time and kept me moving in hope. I would also feel stronger and closer to God there; it was like I would feel and hear God say, "Keep going. I'm with you." And I could have heard His voice in my one-bedroom apartment, but He knew my mind couldn't be still there. That was where I learned environment plays a vital part in the process of transformation and simply hearing and feeling that still small soothing voice of God.

After a year in California, I had the opportunity to move to Atlanta and start a new chapter because of recent changes in the company I was working for at the time, and the timing of it all could not have been more perfect. So I packed up with my son and headed to Atlanta. Before moving to Atlanta, I took a quick trip back to New York for a family gathering at my grandma's house. While there—would you know?—one of favorite cousins let me know he was moving to Atlanta the exact same time I was. If I needed confirmation that I was making the right move for me and my son, that was it.

I just smiled. I was so happy to know how real God's provision was and is as well as listening and knowing God's voice. The beautiful thing about God is he wants intimacy, and the closer you get, the clearer you'll hear his voice, and sometimes you feel this shift in your spirit when he sends certain opportunities that can redirect you or rather put you right back on track. Don't be scared to trust the steps ordered. I wish I could tell you I have prayed about it and that God has shown me what I should do; it's definitely what I will advise someone to do now, but honestly, I truly believe God has blessed my fearlessness, walking by faith that he has something better waiting for me.

I know now that the conviction and knowing I needed to leave was nothing other than the beautiful power of the Holy Spirit. "Now faith is confidence in what we hope for and assurance about what we do not see" (Hebrews 11:1, NIV). "Be strong and courageous. Do not be afraid; do not be discouraged, for the Lord your God will be with you wherever you go" (Joshua 1:9, NIV).

Let me tell you something there was such a divine pour over my state of being on those initial flights, the one from New York to California and that one from California to Atlanta. Both times there was this peace in transition, the calm in change.

Any mother traveling with a baby knows it can be challenging, or so I've heard because I would not know! My baby boy was so calm both times. I felt an ease.

A sign I've learned to look out for when I want to know if this is where I should be or do is peace. God is not a God of confusion, so when you feel peace, that is a sign you're right where you need to be. Now this is not to say you won't be uncomfortable or go through trials, but if you've learned to trust God, He will give you peace in your spirit and joy in your heart that will give the comfort to sustain you through it, "the peace...that surpasses all understanding" (Philippians 4:7, NAB).

So there we were, onto a new chapter. I used to look at my being so open to moving as something I should examine. Maybe it was a sign of inconsistency or fear, and though I was aware one of those moves was made out of fear, most were made out of an unexplainable knowing, my intuition. I know now that it was the presence of the Holy Spirit leading me, never forsaking me, and I'm forever grateful.

Transitioning in Transition

Before I get into my transition physically, it's first important to walk through and reflect on my spiritual transition. As I grow older in wisdom given to me by God, and I praise Him for it, I see how imperative it is to reflect on those turning points, those trials where you might have missed to grab a gem along your wilderness season. Now it's to know that reflecting and regretting are two completely different notions, and I think it's important to make the distinction before I proceed.

Reflecting is looking back to find the good, whether that be hard truths that you have been afraid to face, but now that you're stronger, you're able to look back to see God's provision all up and through that thing because, baby, one thing about God is He is going to come through so hard that you can't miss Him. He has never left you, so sometimes you have to look back before the big breakthrough to recall the whispers God has shared with you then and seeing them manifest through His grace and mercy now.

Now regret is a feeling, a very strong feeling, that creates the perception that what has happened has kept you from what God has in store for you, but what does God's Word say? *"All* things work together for good to those who love God, to those who are the called according to His purpose" (Romans 8:28, NKJV; emphasis mine). So if you took a detour, reflect not only on what has caused it but also on it as a learning tool; then trust and allow God to redirect you and reroute you right where you need to be because he will always. See? I can share the distinction because I, as well as a lot of people, have experienced what these feel like.

Now I used to live in regret a lot, wondering what I could have done differently and why, and it was a revolving door of torment. I'd seen what it could do to someone up close and personal, and it was nothing short of evil.

These days I reflect. *I choose* to take accountability for when I have taken matters into my own hands, and it has caused me pain. It's amazing how we work so hard to get what we want even if we know it isn't good for us but lack the patience when God is working to get us out of the mess we have created. Thank God for his mercy because we'll be lost without it.

My time in Atlanta was interesting. I flew in and saw all the green; there were so many trees. It was beautiful, so calming, and another sign from God that his provision for me was here. My best friend and her family opened her home to me and my son, which was such a beautiful blessing and needed.

I love how God works. Let me now tell you, take some time out of your day every day and reflect on his ways and just smile and say, "I see what you did there." This was definitely one of those times I smiled in amazement.

So during this time, my best friend and I had been building back our friendship after going through the tough season during my pregnancy that we'd both experienced. I want to point that out for a minute because I think it's so important to understand. When we go through hard times with people, always remember you're having an experience, and they're having their own. If we can put ego and pride aside for just a minute and be still, we can allow the grace of God to step in and give mercy to one another.

My best friend and I would talk on the phone while I was living in California, but between the time difference, proximity, and inability to truly connect, it was difficult. And of course, our all-knowing God knew this and created this opportunity in this season of both our lives together. It was just another wonderful testimony revealing that God is love.

I have so many pleasant, fun, beautiful memories of my son and me, my best friend and me, my cousins and me, and all of us together. Looking back, I smile and am so grateful for those times.

To my surprise, Atlanta was nothing I expected and everything I needed. There I was, taking in all that this chapter of the journey had to offer, surrounded by all this nature and the beautiful, thriving black businesses as a black girl; you couldn't help but be inspired and motivated to live out your dreams. The people were so welcoming and warm; as one coming from California, it was such a breath of fresh air.

Though I enjoyed everything Atlanta had to offer, after two years, I couldn't seem to get settled physically and mentally the way I was working toward. My cousins and I traveled to New York a few times to visit. During one of those times, I actually decided to move back to New York for a bit. I was so torn because, although I liked Atlanta, finding work and childcare in a new city was exceptionally hard, not to mention my baby's father was still living in New York, and as my son began to grow, I knew the time would come where having his dad close was vital.

We moved back to New York for about a year, and again, God knew why. During this time, my father had been let go from his job of over thirty years at Merrill Lynch. Bank of America was buying them out, and as they downsized, my father received the short end of the stick and was let go. He took it really hard; it was as if he didn't know just how incredible he was without this job that, from his perspective, defined him all these years. This is and was so difficult to watch because my dad—who was full of energy, talented, and joyous—was experiencing what seemed to be the lowest time of his life.

During this time, my brother and I were constantly reminding him who he was and is for him to take it as an opportunity to choose a new path. Unfortunately, nothing seemed to work. We were noticing nothing was helping him get back to his normal state of mind, so we set out to seek help. He ended up going to his primary doctor, whose clinic was this tiny office right down the block from our home in suburban Hildreth Place in Yonkers. My father explained to the doctor what he'd been feeling—a constant sadness, what he described as a dark pit he couldn't pull himself out of. The doctor proceeded to prescribe my father antidepressants on that first visit, and that was the beginning of the end.

Daddy: Loss, Grief, Guilt, Healing, and Hope

This part of my testimony was difficult to get through. Each time I'd begin writing, so many emotions would come flooding in that I didn't know where to start, but I must share my experience with the best man I had ever known, so I prayed that God would give me the strength in my weakness, and he would do it! So here it goes.

My beautiful, real-life-superhero father, one of my greatest gifts in this life, is Robert William Whyte, a.k.a. Bobby. Bobby was born and raised in Kingston, Jamaica, on September 29, 1959. My dad was abandoned by his biological father as a baby and never knew him. He was raised by his uncle and an amazing community of people in his life over the years he grew. After his mother married, he went to live with her and her husband. My stepfather was a taciturn man, to say the least, very stern; most even called him mean and brutal. Maybe he was misunderstood due to past traumas. I'm not sure, but I only speak of how he showed up in and throughout my father's life.

His stepfather worked at a factory where he got my father a job; each morning they'd have to be there at the same time, but his stepfather would drive and have my father walk. I think that was when my dad figured out that no one hands you anything in life; you have to roll with the punches while holding your head high.

Whenever I'd reflect on my dad's upbringing, I was always amazed at how he can be who he was after going through all that. That's how I know we are a product of our heavenly Father before anyone else's.

From stories I'd gathered of my dad growing up, ones told by others and others shared by him, everyone including my dad would describe him as the man with a plan. He was the person who was friends with everybody, the life of the party. When his friends would come together for a party, he was the grand organizer. My dad had an amazing ear for music and such a beautiful voice. He started a band with a group of talented friends, one of which ended up being my elder brother's godfather later in life. They were called the Devotions, and my dad was the lead singer.

My parents married really young; my mother was eighteen and my dad twenty. They came to America with big dreams, big hopes, and enough love, and with that they built a beautiful life full of warmth, passion, and culture. Like most "perfect" marriages, if you look close enough, you'll see scars and open wounds. My dad and his band would perform and stay out late a lot, while my mother stayed home with my brother, which I understand and now know must have been a terrible feeling of loneliness. Though my father was aware of my mother's loneliness, knowing him, I believe he thought he was doing the right thing for his family. Also, knowing men and my mother, they most likely didn't listen or communicate effectively or as much as they could have.

Looking back, I could see how nerve racking it must have been for my dad stepping into the role of a father. I just never stopped to think about the effect that had on my mother during that time. I think that's because I don't think my mother even spoke about or took her talents seriously enough to build on.

For my father, though, not only did he not have an example since he didn't have one present but he also did not get to fulfill his dreams of becoming a musician. Let me tell you something though; my brother and I would have never known with the type of father he was to us. He loved us, and we knew it; we felt it. My dad was never really affectionate, but that didn't stop his love from being warm, so kind, and safe.

After years of pursuing music, even having the opportunity to open for Beres Hammond, it never happened because my dad always prioritized his family. As much as I am so very grateful for his sacrifices, in hindsight, I wish he didn't. He knew, though, that pursuing a music career full-time and being a great dad and husband was so impossible without one having to suffer, and being the man my father was, he knew that wasn't going to be us. So there he went to hang his dream up, went back to school, and joined the corporate world, working as a financial adviser for one of the most prestigious banks in the world for over twenty-five years.

When my dad first started working in the financial industry, he was so proud that he'd take us on tours of the building during the holidays. Some days when he'd have to go in on the weekend, I'd go with him. I still often smiled at one of my favorite memories of spinning on his office chair, eating all my favorite snacks while waiting for him to done with work for the day. You could see how proud he was and happy it made my father to be in a position to provide above what he could have possibly imagined for his family growing up.

After nearly thirty years of working for this company, my father was let go, just like that! Being a vital part of this growing company in which he invested his time and efforts for as many years of his life, being let go was the beginning of what broke my father. Seeing my father's light dwindle each day after losing his job shook our world to the core!

After struggling with the feelings that came along with the transition of change and loss, we went to see a doctor. After that initial appointment, my dad went alone to a follow-up. During that appointment, the doctor referred my dad to a psychiatrist who, without hesitation, prescribed an antidepressant. That time of our lives was a complete blur; before we could even process what my father was experiencing, he was already prescribed three to four different antidepressants. The biggest regret of my life was not being more involved, more educated, and more assertive during that process.

Oftentimes we as people, especially black people, take a doctor's word without asking the necessary questions. I'd look back at our experience and see how they looked at this vulnerable black man experiencing pain that could have been identified and treated with talking therapy, but no one took the time. By the time my father started with talking therapy, his chemistry was already altered through the prescribed antidepressants.

My father battled heavily with this depression for four years. In the beginning, my brother and I would encourage him every chance we could. I would massage him, give him baths, and do whatever I thought would help remind him how loved he was and how important he was to us. The fourth year was difficult; it seemed like nothing was working.

I'd look back at this year and become extremely emotional because it was a hard reality for me when I realized I didn't show my father that same tender love he deserved up until the last minute of his earthly life. It was a year that affected my entire life; I'd wept in my brokenness to God in humility, wishing I did things differently. You see, I thought we'd been trying tender love, but maybe tough love would work, so I would say things like, "Only you can get yourself out of this dark hole!" I began to make what my father was going through about me, which was the worst choice of my life.

The enemy took full advantage of our vulnerability and lack of knowledge. All this hurt from past trauma started to surface, feelings of being unprotected and unhealed. I used to carry shame as a result of allowing the enemy used my pain during a time where all we could feel was pain. I started hearing questions like "Who was there for me when I was hurting? I've been depressed my entire life, and no one ever tried to help or rescue me!" They were valid and real feelings but completely selfish thinking; it was not the time to deal with them, which was how I knew now that it was the enemy.

The enemy knew what needed to evoke in our lives by using my past hurt and my father's to steal, kill, and destroy. Letting him fulfill his plan will always be my deepest hurt, but I know *my* heavenly Father, *who is both mine and my earthly father's Father, will restore.* I only wished I understood that then.

My dad would constantly say to us, "You don't understand," and he was right. The fear of not knowing what to do made me hard and cold. I was so engulfed in my pain while watching my hero go through so much pain, and nothing was working. I was lost; I wanted my father to have hope, but I know now it was impossible without God. We needed to lean into him and rely on him and him alone for healing.

After exhausting everything we could to help my father with healing and seeing the horrible effects of the medication on my father's body—everything from insomnia to diarrhea, anxiety, and constipation—I decided to research a natural herbalist to help detox and rid his body of these medications that were killing him. We knew it was what needed to be done. Little did we know, during the consultation, that the herbalist would inform us that due to the body and mind now being regulated by the antidepressants, stopping them would send his body in complete shock and possibly kill him. I left that appointment feeling defeated and out of options.

One day I woke up and decided my baby boy needed a new environment, so I asked my mom and sister to pick us up for the weekend. As I drove off, I looked my father in the eyes while he was standing in the backyard; that would be the last time I looked my father in the eyes. Every time I remembered that moment, it felt intense and heavy and I didn't know if that was the weight it held after losing him, but it was in the slowest motion.

I planned to stay at my mom's just for the weekend with my son. The next morning I woke up to a phone call from my brother telling me he was with our father in the bathroom. My father hung himself early that morning, and my brother found him. I'd get a paralyzing chill whenever I thought of what that felt like for my brother because, for me, the pain of losing my father was an emptiness that held no words. So I could never imagine what my brother felt and feels.

The car ride from my mother's house to my home, to my dad, was the longest car ride of my life. When we arrived on the block, there was traffic due to the ambulance and police. I got out of the car and ran for my life up the stairs on my home, only to find out my father was already on the way to the hospital.

When we arrived at the hospital, we waited for hours, but I just knew he'd be OK. He couldn't die, not like this, not without me saying I loved him one last time, not without me saying I was sorry for not being stronger, not without me hugging him, kissing him, smelling him, and sitting on his lap one last time.

The doctor walked into the room we were waiting in, and she just shook her head no. Everything went blank.

The loss of my father left me emotionally, mentally, and spiritually crippled for a very long time. I was lost. I had no idea what was next for my life.

Grief is such a deep, disheartening, interesting experience. The best I can do to describe the unique journey of grief is to compare it to a deep, cold ocean. It comes in waves and rushes in depending on the current.

I think what hurt the most was that life kept moving on without him here. *How?* I just knew my children would grow up laughing at his jokes and jamming to all the old soul music when they were with him. I just knew he'd be here to walk me down the aisle one day.

I want to encourage anyone who is dealing with depression themselves or knows someone who is. *Love them.* Love them gently, listen to them, be there for them, hold them as much as you can, and support them, but the biggest takeaway I want anyone reading this to have is that *it is impossible to fight through spiritual warfare without the full armor of God.* "For we do not wrestle against flesh and blood, but against principalities, against powers, against the rulers of the darkness of this age, against spiritual *hosts* of wickedness in the heavenly *places*" (Ephesians 6:12, NKJV).

"Do not be afraid or discouraged because of this vast army. For the battle is not yours, but God's" (2 Chronicles 20:15, NIV).

After losing my father, I felt nothing was there for me in New York. I needed to get away from any and everything that reminded me of the pain of losing him. I needed to run, so I did. After some time in New York, I made the decision to move back to Atlanta for a bit while I figured out what was next.

Unfortunately when we run away from circumstances we should be working through, the Holy Spirit will always guide us back to where we should have never left to begin with and will do it with strength and grace. So because I wasn't making the decision willingly, I was hit with a trial that would redirect me. An unexpected incident happened that put me in financial difficulties, and I knew I could no longer afford my bills with what I now had in my savings, so I had to make a decision and fast.

Hometown Bound

I sat there on a Greyhound bus leaving Atlanta, cuddled up with my son, on our way back to New York, making sure we had everything we needed to limit the amount of times we had to get off. It would have been ideal to fly, but I needed to save every penny to help build our new life. Moving back to New York, though I knew it was exactly where my son and I needed to be, definitely took some adjusting to. Here I was, with my and son me against the world in the past few years, moving back to my mother's house.

At this point, I hadn't lived with my mother since the age of fourteen, so I wasn't sure what to expect. I was so excited of the possibility of rebuilding a relationship with my mother and to spend some quality time with my baby sister, whom I missed beyond words! I was also excited for my son to build a stronger, closer relationship with his father, one they both deserved.

So while the trial of moving back felt extremely uncomfortable, I knew it was the step in the right direction.

To be honest, the day I discovered that the only option was to move back to New York, I felt an immense sense of relief. God is a perfect God. With Nas starting school that same year and getting older, God knew I needed a trial to reveal what I knew needed to happen all along.

When I arrived in New York, I spent the first six months getting us acclimated. There wasn't much space for us at my mother's, but we all did the best we could. Within the next two years, I'd be living out suitcases and saving up enough to find a place for us. Any New Yorker knows that finding an apartment in a good neighbor-hood with good schools and a good environment is no easy task, and I just saw time passing by.

I would say, though, the amount of joy and peace I felt in getting to live in the same house as my sister. For the first time as young women, my sister and I spent nights staying up, talking all night, doing each other's hair. We had late nights and early morning walks together. I often believe God sent me there for us to have that time again, and I'm so grateful for the blessing it truly was. I also was able to see my brother, whom I was missing like crazy for years, as well as my cousins, my aunt, and everybody. I didn't realize just how much I needed those moments to fill my soul.

Seeing my son with his father was another one of those things. I saw how happy they both were. My son was surrounded by the most love from family that he'd ever experienced thus far, and it would melt me every time I'd see and think of the blessing it was.

Mothers, especially single mothers, I know it can be hard to believe our babies need more than us, but they absolutely do, and here's the good news—so do you. That's the beautiful way God has designed it; it truly takes a village. Our children need the most love, words of wisdom, inspiration, and exposure to new beautiful, memorable experiences; again, I know it's hard to accept, but it won't always include us, and that's OK. It's more than OK; it is a blessing from our heavenly Father.

Back at my mother's house, we lived with her husband, who was the reason I moved out when I was fourteen to begin with. He made the atmosphere heavy, to say the least, and I just did everything I could to stay out of his way. As a grown woman with her son, it was the last experience I wanted for us while back at my mother's house but there was no space for expectations. I just knew what needed to be done and did it. Get my son registered for school and find a job and that I did.

One Friday morning as I was getting my son ready for school, my mother informed me that her husband had guests coming to the house to stay indefinitely and that my son and I needed to be out that same weekend. Now you can imagine the amount of anxiety and fear that came over my body in that moment. I had no clue what I was going do. I tried so hard to hide my emotions from my son as we were on our way to school that morning, but it was not an easy task. So I tried my best to keep our routine the same.

On Friday mornings we'd stop at Dunkin' Donuts before school, but this morning wasn't like any other morning. As I was on the line, everything just went into slow motion. I was looking at my son in amazement that God blessed me to be his mom, and a great feeling of hope consumed me. I immediately scooped my son up into my arms and began to cry. It was safe to say everyone in Dunkin' Donuts was probably looking at me like I was crazy, but it was only us in that room. Shortly after, something miraculous happened. My cousin walked in.

As many times as I'd frequented this Dunkin' Donuts, I had never run into my cousin who, by the way, lived relatively close by, but this morning he happened to walk in. I would always have a sweet spot in my heart for Dunkin' Donuts, as silly as it may sound. Anyway, my cousin took one look at me and proceeded to ask me what was going on. I explained everything to him, and he let me know in that moment that I could come and stay with him for however long I needed to.

I couldn't believe it. I was in complete awe because I knew a turn of events like that was nothing other than God! So as soon as I could, I packed up our things and moved them all to my cousin's house. That weekend was a whirlwind, to say the least.

We stayed with my cousin for about a year; although I was in no way naive to the huge blessing it was, I'd be lying if I didn't mention just how much of a humbling experience it was moving in with my younger cousin at that point in my life. It taught me just how much humility played a major role in those pivotal times along the journey. So there I was, sleeping on a twin-sized bed, cuddled with my son, and still able to clearly see that God was still at work in my life. Knowing and feeling that truth was all the hope I needed to keep going.

At the time, my cousin and his fiancée were also expecting a baby. So as his family was growing, my move-out date was on a visible time frame. As I worked and saved up, looking for an apartment just became more and more of a struggle. My cousin and I discussed a date, and what do you know? I found an apartment in the same week as that date for less than the price I needed. I couldn't believe it. It was a small apartment but a huge blessing, and I embraced that apartment with an immense amount of humility and gratitude because I knew it was only by the grace of God that things were falling into place the way they were.

> Some may look and call it small, but they don't understand. No, they don't understand at all.

> Out of the dark that you've brought me through, I praise your name, knowing it was only possible with you.

After two to three months of being there, my son's father let me know of this two-bedroom apartment that his uncle owned and had just become available, which was three times the size of my apartment for the same amount I was paying. It was nothing short of a miracle because while I was so grateful for our little apartment, the option to give my son more made it an easy one. It reminded me of God's plans for us and how he always wants to give us more of the very best quality.

The move happened so fast and effortlessly that I was in absolute amazement of how God was working in my life. Moving was an easy decision, my son went up a couple of nights before me to stay with his father, while I focused on packing us up for the move. That ride uptown in the U-Haul holding all our belongings and onto a new journey, on the way to our new home, felt as if I were surrounded by heavenly angels. The minute I walked into our new home, I knew I was home, and this was the place where we'd truly begin to build our life.

The Birthright of the Creator's Creation:
Created by the Creator to Create

Creativity is such a beautiful gift from God that is a part of our nature, of our very being. I'd never given myself a ceiling to my creativity; I just always felt that God had gifted me with all these talents—writing, singing, and keen attention to detail—to one day use it all for his glory. I never was one who was scared to dream, to start over if necessary, or to hope because I always had this knowing that there was always more. Along the way, I know that, for some of us, dreaming has been stifled by this capitalistic, oppressive system that we've missed the knowing of this oh-so-beautiful expression and manifestation of creativity.

While giving this chapter a title, it brought up the many limitations we put on ourselves whether consciously or subconsciously. The enemy would deceive us with lies through shame, guilt or anger, I started to notice the strongholds and the effects it had on and throughout my life. As I looked back on my childhood and things I'd witnessed growing up, especially from some women in my family, I saw it was a generational curse I needed to be set free from. Praise God we are free in Christ Jesus! Now I need to free my mind, emotions, and creativity every day by choosing and surrendering to Christ, aware I cannot do it alone, nor do I have to. Amen for that!

If you were born in the '80s or '90s, majority of your parents sadly did not have the "luxury" to dream. Dreaming takes, our true reality requires faith. So when you really think about it, the American dream has completely stripped our ancestors of the knowing of relying on God, and the saddest part is that we've allowed it. We've allowed our circumstance to determine not only our future but also our mind and identity. Now that's not to say I don't understand how, and here's how. You present fear wrapped in limited options and resources, making it impossible to learn and grow. Unfortunately as black people, we've experienced the result of the "how" for far too long. The enemy uses noise and corruption to keep us from the steadfast, faithful, Almighty God, and I believe Christians of this generation, young and old, are here to partner with God to restore the dream.

The truth is there is only one true dream, and that is of the kingdom; once we know we are heavenly beings experiencing the earth, we live fearlessly, and the enemy knew it. So instead, he invented one of the biggest scams of all called the American dream, a limited dream, when we should be trusting in the One who provides. "'For my thoughts are not your thoughts, neither are your ways my ways,' declares the Lord. 'As the heavens are higher than the earth, so are my ways higher than your ways and my thoughts than your thoughts'" (Isaiah 55:8–9, NIV).

Can you imagine being so oppressed that there is no room to hope for more? It is being given a limit that is beneath what you're destined for, and the worst of all is believing it.

Our Creator, who knew us and his perfect plan for our lives both collectively and individually before the foundation of this world, wants us to trust that plan! It's so easy to get distracted in this world because there are so many factors and obstacles intentionally placed along our journey to keep us from fulfilling our divine plan. The beauty is our heavenly Father isn't asking for us to figure it out all on our own.

This world will have you think the formula to success and prosperity, which we all want, is to hustle with no days off and nonstop grind. This, in actuality, contradicts what *the Lawgiver* says. First, the only reason why we desire success and prosperity is that we have been created by a God of abundance and prosperity. So of course, those desires will naturally be a part of our spirit. We spend forty-plus hours of our time a week working for someone else who tells us what they'll be paying us, only to be overworked and left striving for an unattainable goal when, in reality, our birthright is higher than what we're working so hard for. The problem is just like everything else: the enemy has found ways to pervert a God thing by deceiving us to think it's a "good thing."

Ask yourself, what are you striving for? Is it money? Is it success? Is it to be loved by people? Is it to help people? God tells us the formula to anything in life. "Seek ye first the kingdom of God, and his righteousness; and all these things shall be added unto you" (Matthew 6:33, KJV).

I've learned to consult the Lord in helping me walk the steps he has ordered for me, and to do that, I needed to trust in Him completely. While the enemy cannot create, he's very much aware that because we are created in the image of God, we are here and able to create. A tactic of the enemy is suggesting false narratives and ideas that can lead us astray from our destiny, which is why God's Word is imperative to our walk in this life.

> "Trust in the Lord with all your heart, And lean not on your own understanding; In all your ways acknowledge Him, And He shall direct your paths" (Proverbs 3:5–6, NKJV). Trusting in God teaches me patience more and more every day and to wait on the Lord for instruction and guidance for me to know what is for me and what is sent by the enemy to detour me from what is for me. "Wait for the Lord; be strong and take heart and wait for the Lord" (Psalm 27:14, NIV).

My mind used to be so preoccupied with the thought of failing at what I wanted to do with my life that I'd often miss my life as it was happening. I decided very early on that music was what I wanted to do with my life, and I couldn't see anything else as a possibility. The way music made me feel was something out of this world; it consumed me.

I discovered my singing voice at around age eleven; my brother and I would sit up all night, freestyling music. He'd play his acoustic guitar, and I'd sing my big heart out; nothing made me happier. When I entered high school, I met other creatives who loved music and singing as much as I did; not only did I become inspired by fellow creatives but I was also experiencing more of life and evolving as a young woman. Around my sophomore year, I started to incorporate my poetry into my music, which turned into me discovering my ability to rap. From there I was hooked, and music was my fix. I'd lose sleep thinking of all the ways I would one day make my dreams come true, so much so that the thought of me not "making it" would bring me to tears.

All my teenage years, my twenties, and my very early thirties were dedicated to becoming a successful mainstream musical artist while holding a nine-to-five to make sure I was providing for my responsibilities including and most importantly my son once he was born. From countless studio sessions to music videos, networking events, and strategizing, all my efforts were put into my dream, but something happened: life began to change; therefore, I began to change. During this time in my life, I always followed my intuition. I loved that about me. It's amazing how you don't appreciate the beautiful characteristics about yourself that make you uniquely you until the day you look up, and you've become a shadow of that person.

Once I lost my dad, everything changed for me. The pain of losing my daddy the way I did catapulted me into a new meaning of my purpose in the world. I knew that no one makes it through losing a parent to suicide without becoming a part of the solution. From that point on, my dreams in music felt like child's play, and though I couldn't see how life was supposed to go on without my dad, what I did know was that it could not and would not ever be the same. Though I would still make music often, the passion I had for it was no longer there.

I started reflecting on the days my brother and friends would stay up countless nights creating music, which would oftentimes turn into all-night discussions about music just being the foundation of building generational wealth that could help and build our community. In hindsight, I see how God's hand was putting all the pieces back together even as life removed and reshaped them. He is the Almighty, Grand Architect.

From New Age Back to the Same God Today, Tomorrow, and Forever

A child losing their daddy to antidepressants is nothing short of traumatizing. I was desperately seeking to bring awareness to mental health and a preventive fix to avoid anyone having to experience seeing someone they love fade away and suffer the way my amazing, wonderful father had.

In 2019 a friend and I set out to start a business focused on natural healing. March 2020 was always the set date; little did we know that year would be the beginning of something we could have never imagined. The world shut down. Life as we knew it was over, set aside at a standstill. Nonetheless, we were determined to stick to the plan, thinking we'd keep it close and monitored, just close family and friends.

My business partner was someone with whom I'd been around for over fifteen years but never really formed a friendship. Her brother and my brother were like best friends since high school, and though we'd always shown love to each other when we'd cross paths, that would be the extent of our relationship at the time. Once we started to build a friendship that in 2019, we saw that we had a lot of pain in common; some would call that trauma bonding. I honestly really dislike the term *trauma bonding* because I think it diminishes the complexity of pain. Pain is so deep and complex with many layers.

I believe due to God's grace, he knew we were not depending on him as we should have at the time, so he needed to get creative. He placed both of us in that season to have our pain reflect each other, though in different lights but in the same need of wanting to feel seen and understood and a need to help others who felt the same. We provided that emotional support for each other not because we had that deep of a friendship but because we recognized that pain in each other, which made us identify a real need.

This led to us wanting to go into the business of natural healing. We saw the need and lack of resources in our communities and wanted to be a part of the solution. It had been something that was on our hearts for a while, so when we came together and noticed we had a lot of similar ideas, we felt it was then meant to be.

We spent the year of 2019 planning, and in the middle to the end of that year, we planned our grand opening of the Wellness House of Healing. It'd be a wellness space of natural healers serving the community with our gifts and talents we'd learned and perfected over the years.

At this time we were going to different networking events and pop-up shops to promote the opening. I began to entertain a lot of rituals and ideologies I never did before this chapter of my life, specifically because my father would always tell me, "Once you open a door and allow something in, you're allowing something in," and that always stuck with me. Nonetheless, there I was amid tarot readers, yogis, Reiki healers, and people professing to be spiritual with no reverence or knowledge of *the true Spirit* and *God* in heaven, myself included. I said that because I wasn't acting like it; you see, being in this environment at the time affected my fear of God, which breaks my heart to admit. When you begin to feel empowered by something other than the divine spirit, like my father said those many years ago, you allow something in that isn't of God, and if it isn't of God, it is the enemy.

"No one can serve two masters. Either you will hate the one and love the other" (Matthew 6:24, NIV). "Thou shalt have no other gods before me" (Exodus 20:3, KJV). When we subscribe to anything as our source of power, healing, or strength that is not of God, we are choosing against God. During that time, I handed the enemy access in so many ways, being influenced by others who weren't influenced by Jesus Christ, and it was no one else's fault but my own.

Spring of 2020 had been the set date to open the Wellness House of Healing to the community, and though it was very rewarding seeing our vision come to fruition, it was during a time that would forever change our world. While taking all the necessary precautions, we decided to move forward with the opening because we believed the need was far more important than the fear. While opening a business during the height of COVID-19, I was surrounded by all this new energy, some welcomed and most subconsciously not welcomed.

This season brought up a lot of suppressed pain from losing my dad that came flooding in overpowering waves. I began indulging in marijuana heavily. Now I would smoke here and there, but in efforts to numb the pain, I'd run through an eight-pack in a day by myself easily, and for any nonsmoker, let's just say that was a lot!

I also began masturbating, which I really hadn't done since I was a lot younger. At the time I thought, "Hey, I'm single, living on my own. I'd have my alone time. Why not?" But I knew it was something extremely wrong because of the shame and sadness I'd feel immediately after.

I would go into this trancelike state, and in hindsight, I knew there was something demonic happening in my home; through masturbation I unknowingly invited them in. Then I'd smoke again to numb the shame, so there I was, the founder of a business whose mission was to help heal others in pain, while I was home alone, drowning in it. The thing was no one around me knew; looking back, I realized it was a pain that resonated with me—that feeling of going through pain alone and being surrounded by all these people who couldn't see it. "You keep track of all my sorrows. You have collected all my tears in your bottle. You have recorded each one in your book" (Psalm 56:8, NLT).

I know now that the true natural divine healing is first accepting Jesus Christ as your personal Savior, and from there the Holy Spirit will lead us into all truth. *What is a delay to us is perfect timing. God works outside of time; we have no idea. The Bible says time is a talent. What will we do with it?*

Looking to cover my pain, I stayed busy. I was inspired with the idea of starting a podcast with some other dope creatives I knew, and that was exactly what we did. The podcast was titled *Black Axis*, where we spoke on topics that directly affected our people, black people. There has always been a war on black lives, and instead of just talking about it among ourselves, we proactively wanted to be a part of the solution. We addressed overcoming oppression, political views, and generational trauma.

Now before I continue, as a black woman, I must say being born into a world where black people has been ostracized, beaten down spiritually and physically, brutally murdered, and violently oppressed, among other experiences I don't believe words can even express, I know now, especially after going through this experience, that as much as we can point out the pure evil of capitalism and government and the oppression of black people, who are the original people and such a powerful force, others are threatened by what we can do and have done. The oppression of my beautiful people is a cruelty I will never understand in its entirety while here on the earth. I began to think of all the other cruelties I would never understand, like *anyone* being murdered, pedophilia, a mother losing a child to violence, and rape. I could go on and on. It brought me back to the Garden of Eden and God placing a tree of good and evil.

God is the only one who is good (Mark 10:18), and we also know God is love. Love in purest form is God. So what is evil? Who is evil? How do we identify evil if we cannot see it for what it truly is? The Bible tells us of the enemy who has come to deceive the whole world (Revelation 12:9). Now if deception needs truth to deceive, how then can we know good from evil? A truth from a lie?

We saw and experienced both in its true form. Though I believe Adam and Eve were taught about good and evil, it was not in God's plan that we'd experience evil, but through Christ Jesus, we are granted another opportunity to get it right. Hallelujah!

In Christ setting us free from true bondage, we can one day experience the life God has intended for us. I often wonder if, in seeing bondage, we can better understand it not only physically but also spiritually and mentally. We know from God's Word that He'll never give us more than we can bear. I believe and know we black people are the *only* group of people who can have this unique experience and somehow produce more resilience than we already have—to praise God through the pain, to find hope in environments meant to evoke hopelessness, to have victory over obstacles put in place for us to lose, and to build and share love when we've been hated.

As I began to seek God, I felt this pull, this knowing. As much as I loved what we were creating in the podcast, God's presence was not there. We were a few episodes in, and we hadn't released anything yet, and now I know that was another one of God's divine delays. I continued feeling that pull, not sure what it was at the time. (Now I know it was the conviction and guidance of the Holy Spirit.)

One night while recording, I was frozen with conviction. God was never a part of our discussions/topics nor acknowledging Jesus Christ as the remedy, the way, the truth, and the life. I forgot what the topic was; again, I was so still from the voice of God in the moment. All I heard was one of my cast members and friend opposing the question. "What about faith?" I just stopped and said. Yep, that was all I needed.

I've never told her this, but I truly thank her for allowing God to use her because that was exactly what happened in that moment. God knew her as brilliant, outspoken, and confident, and she'd say whatever he put on her heart to share, and I'm forever grateful she did. You see how much God knows just who to use and how much he loves us?

The next day I felt this strong conviction to send out a book of a text message in our podcast group chat, saying I couldn't be a part of something that doesn't point to Jesus Christ as the solution because he is the only way! I voiced that I wanted my role in the podcast to acknowledge Jesus Christ as the answer, the only hope, the solution to everything we were discussing and seeking. It was safe to say I was left on read, chile.

I know that everyone read that text like, "What is this girl talking 'bout? She's bugged." And guess what, I couldn't care less because the peace of the Holy Spirit came over the minute I hit Send; it was incomparable. I know through my obedience that God was pleased, and I felt accomplished like, "OK, God, I did it, What's next?" And let me tell you, there was a lot that was next. I had work to do, and the Holy Spirit led me straight to that work. Now before this, I felt as if I was just coasting through, making strides in my entrepreneurial journey but lacking spiritually.

When I set out on my spiritual relationship by cultivating my relationship with the Most High God, the more I learned, the more peace of knowing came on me. I was forced to no longer be comfortable at coasting. Here was where the fight began.

This season was my closet time, my alone time with God. I felt extremely blessed and loved that God wanted this time with me. Me?

As I reflect, I'm reminded of an Ellen G. White writing from *The Ministry of Healing* that one of my best friends has brought to my attention just the other day. It's a story of a caged bird. It reads:

In the full light of day, and in hearing of the music of other voices, the caged bird will not sing the song that his master seeks to teach him. He learns a snatch of this, a trill of that, but never a separate and entire melody. But the master covers the cage, and places it where the bird will listen to the one song he is to sing. In the dark, he tries and tries again to sing that song until it is learned, and he breaks forth in perfect melody. Then the bird is brought forth, and ever after he can sing that song in the light. Thus God deals with His children. He has a song to teach us, and when we have learned it amid the shadows of affliction we can sing it ever afterward.

I began to read and study the Bible for myself for the very first time in my life. I began to feel how much the Word was alive and transforming me daily, rapidly, minute to minute, second by second, but the work had only just begun.

I began to purge my apartment of any and everything the Holy Spirit led me to. Little did I know that, while I was purging my home, God was doing some pruning of His own in other areas of my life.

My business partner informed me that she was packing up and moving to Africa. You know when you hear people say that something has thrown them for a loop? The news of this did just that, not to mention we were already feeling overwhelmed with managing to keep things afloat before I received the news. I thought, "How am I going to keep a business intended to be a collective one running on my own?" Although it brought all the physical feelings of anxiety in, I also had this peace in my spirit that God was doing a great work, and as the weeks went by, I started to see it.

Because of the wellness business, I was engulfed in all these outside sources such as "healing" crystals, sun god artwork, and artwork promoting chakra "healing." These are all works of the devil; they are idolatry, witchcraft, and dangerous. That's how deception works. Remember earlier when I mentioned deception cannot be without some truth so it may feel good, like it provided healing, but it actually does the opposite?

The agenda of the enemy is and has always been for those greater than him to worship him. He tried it with Jesus, and since Christ was God on the earth, though in human form, he commanded Satan to get behind, and he fled.

That old serpent knows that though our spirit is willing, our flesh is weak. So he deceives us with these false idols and false sources of energy to attain your worship by any means necessary. As one of my homegirls puts it, "He's cheap!"

See, our adversary forces; our *King* Jesus gives us freely as well as gives us the power to choose *him* freely. So my message to you is do not be deceived, brothers and sisters, for it only leads to bondage. Choose freedom; choose Christ Jesus because he sacrificed it all for you. That should let us know not only that we are loved beyond the capacity of this world but also just how amazing God's plan is for our lives from the beginning of Creation.

A beautiful revelation in my testimony during this time was one of my favorites in my journey. Opening the door to new age practices came with a lot of false teachings, which the Holy Spirit had to expose and rid my soul, spirit, and environment of. One of those lingering portals was angel numbers; I would often see a number and google it for meaning and guidance. The Holy Spirit began to impress on my heart and pour out wisdom, leading me into all truth, and that did not include the deception of angel numbers.

I drove home one day, and I looked up and saw the time being 10:10 a.m. At this point I had been seeing the number 10:10 very often—so often that I knew it had to be a message. For a second I thought to go to Google to look into the meaning of 10:10 in angel numbers, but something in my spirit said, "Stop!" God presented the question to me. "Do you trust me? Am I not enough?"

It immediately made me emotional and stopped me in my tracks, and I responded, "Yes, Lord, I trust you!" I never looked to angel numbers as a source ever again after that.

The next day I was driving again, and on my first time looking at the time, what time did I see? You guessed it—10:10. I looked down at my phone for another confirmation to just smile in awe at how frequently I'd been seeing this number. I had this knowing that it was a message, not knowing what it was, but the divine fact that God was sending me a message was enough for me to smile with joy. What happened next always made me emotional.

I had the Bible app downloaded on my cell phone, and the app had updated daily Bible verses and sent them as a pop-up message. As I was holding my phone in my hand, the Bible verse for the day popped up, and it was *John 10:10*! "The thief comes only to steal and kill and destroy. I came that they may have life and have it abundantly" (ESV). I was yet again in absolute awe and amazement of how God showed me what would be revealed if I trusted and waited on him, and that was he would constantly reveal with love and authority his plan and purpose for my life. I'd been seeing 10:10, and each time I did, I was filled with joy not because I needed the meaning, not because I knew the direction but because I knew the Source. "I will give you a new heart and put a new spirit in you; I will remove from you your heart of stone and give you a heart of flesh" (Ezekiel 36:26, NIV).

A year after that strong conviction, my life took another unexpected turn for the better though it took me by surprise. I found out I was pregnant with my second child, my baby girl. This time around was so different and yet alike in a lot of ways. I always envisioned my life as most women do—you know, married, then come children—but there we were on our second child, unmarried and very much still growing in this twenty year + relationship. I have to admit, for the sake of transparency and blessing someone else through my story, that I wasn't sure having another baby was something I could do and was ready for. My children's father and I were working out how we would walk into the future, whether together forever as a family or separate, whichever would be healthier for our family.

Our relationship was like a flower that no one tended to, being kept in a dark closet with no light and no water. We were too comfortable yet so uncomfortable to stretch, comfortable in being stagnant, but God was working behind the scenes yet again. We were so unwilling to do the necessary work and so unaware, as we often are, that the almighty Gardener was watering our flower as we experienced it as being uncomfortable while being stretched as we grew, not knowing we were being nourished all along.

Our relationship was growing, but so was I—mentally, emotionally, and of course physically. I was crying out to God for strength and for guidance on what I should do.

Out of my mind with emotions from hormones and fear, I scheduled an appointment to explore "my options," but God wouldn't have it. An unexpected blizzard hit that closed every facility for three days straight. Though I already knew, in that moment God confirmed that this baby was a beautiful blessing sent from him, and while it may be hard, he would be with me every step of the way, and that he was!

The first few months for me were extremely difficult, to say the least. I experienced terrible morning sickness, and mentally I was really struggling. Looking back now, I saw how much God was pressing me into something/someone new, not a new me who disregarded all the pain and trauma but a new me who embraced my victory in Christ and knew I am me because of what I'd been through. "Neither do men put new wine into old bottles: else the bottles break, and the wine runneth out, and the bottles perish: but they put new wine into new bottles, and both are preserved" (Matthew 9:17, KJV).

The process of becoming had been painful and uncomfortable, and while I was terrified in what my life would look like being a single mother of two, I also had this peace and knowing in my spirit that the same God who had provided for me through the impossible was the God who was here with me now. Trusting God had been the best decision of my life. Through trusting him, I had two amazing, healthy, beautiful children; through trusting Him, it forced that flower (my relationship) into the light, through trusting Him I have grown and continue to grow in unimaginable ways.

My children's father and I were faced with all the conversations we'd been coasting by for years, and instead of us wanting to live our best lives separately, God revealed that He has placed us together over twenty + years ago for a reason, and it was time for us to truly seek out all the reasons why. It had been an uncomfortable yet beautiful journey; not only did it bring up all our "stuff" to the surface but individually we also were blown away at the mirror we held up to one another. It revealed all the ugly things we hid away, hoping no one would find. From there, we began to enter into this divine territory that helped us grow and until this day God continues to help us flourish.

You see, it is truly amazing how our Creator works. While I'm well aware everyone's testimony is different and unique in its own way, I come to see how often God hides the miracles in a package that is quite unappealing.

It makes me think of how we have been given the best gift—Jesus Christ.

Here was our Lord and Savior, the King of kings, coming into humanity to save us, and how did our Father send him? He sent him as a baby, born in a barn surrounded by animals. This is *the King* of the universe (heaven and earth) we're talking about! He was born to a mother and father no one deemed as extraordinary. I love how God works! His ways are so beautiful because, through His plans, we can spend years peeling back the gems, the lessons we learn through the trials on the way to the promise. I love that we serve a brilliant, all-knowing, marvelous, almighty, healing, providing, merciful, graceful, loving, caring, hilarious, restoring, replenishing, abundant God.

Me versus Me

After giving birth to my beautiful baby girl, I felt complete, but I also struggled a lot mentally. I weighed the most I had in my entire life, I was home all the time, and I went back to work a little over a month after giving birth, which was the most horrible decision. I began eating my emotions, and I didn't notice it was a problem until I looked in the mirror and didn't recognize myself. I cried in private—often. I felt so ashamed; here I was, knowing how incredibly blessed I was to have these beautiful children and a growing relationship, but I also felt like I was drowning in a sea of emotions. I hated that I didn't feel stable and happy; I was just hoping no one noticed while hoping someone would so I could be rescued from my own body working against me. The feelings were complex and overbearing.

In addition to the hormones that came along postpartum, I always feared bringing another child into the world. I just didn't think I was fully capable of being the mother I truly wanted to be. I began allowing questions to stir me up, but never would I let them come up enough where I'd have to face them. I know now that in doing that, not only was I not living in authenticity but by suppressing these feelings, it was acting as poison to my being as well. I'd notice a pattern in my choices, and I'd often ask, "Would I make the same choices willingly had my innocence not been perverted against my will?"

You see, I come to learn that by neglecting these questions, you'll never get to the root. This wasn't about my abuse, my guilt, my shame, or my insecurity. This was about the freedom of my will that the enemy came to steal, and I had to fight for my life to take back what was *mine*. God had freely given me the freedom of choice, and I wasn't going to let a loser come and take that from me, no matter how hard he tried!

I started to look at the reality of the situation called my life, and in doing that, I realized I didn't know myself. I got teary eyed even writing that now, but it was the truth.

It's a scary place to look in the mirror and know that you're beautiful, kind to people, creative, funny, talented, and able to acknowledge wonderful things about yourself but not see it clearly. It's like it's hidden behind this fog, and that fog of a facade hid me, not allowing myself to truly be seen by me. Wild, huh? It wasn't until I began to seek, remember, and learn more about just how much God loved me that I began to see myself clearly.

After groaning all my ugly truths in prayer, the questions to myself began to change. I began asking myself, "If God loves me so much, enough to experience excruciating pain in the garb of this physical realm, so that I may one day see eternal life and, better yet, get to meet him?" But wait, there's more! He loves me enough to rescue me when I need him. He wants a personal relationship with me, a friendship, a father-and-daughter relationship. He wants to work with me and wants me to work with him—now. If the Creator of all things, including me, loves me this much, the question starts to be, How could I not love me?

So, beloved, fight for your life! For it is truly *for your life*. God has instilled everything you need, and most importantly you already have the victory through Jesus Christ, our King, so run to Him for cover. Put on your whole armor and let this world know who's boss! Shine that light so the Giver of light may be revealed through the darkness.

If you look up the word *fear*, you'll find a number of meanings. The root word of *fear* has many meanings attached to it such as sudden danger, peril, harm, distress, and deception. To me, researching fear was so interesting because the feeling alone was at times difficult to put into words.

"The weapons we fight with are not the weapons of the world. On the contrary, they have divine power to demolish strongholds. We demolish arguments and every pretension that sets itself up against the knowledge of God, and we take captive every thought to make it obedient to Christ. And we will be ready to punish every act of

disobedience, once your obedience is complete"
(2 Corinthians 10:4–6, NIV).

I wrote a song recently that went, "My fear was my security." And, baby, was it! I felt paralyzed by it. I would always hear that "the mind is a battlefield." It wasn't until I got older and was able to discern past and present feelings that I truly identified that statement as true. I would often think something was wrong with me.

The worst thing about spiritual warfare, aside from the fact that you're fighting the fight of your life in a realm you cannot see, is the cruel, distorted perversion that seeps into the mind, and I feel that it happens not only subconsciously but consciously as well. The difference is, consciously, I choose to stand in the victory of my Lord and Savior, Jesus Christ. Putting on the full armor of God is the only way you and I will combat it. Trust me. Trust God. Trust me as I trust God!

It's truly amazing to me how the mind works. You know that list of things we wish we could change about ourselves? Or is it just me? Well, mine would definitely have to be my overthinking. I listen to myself at times, trying to control my mind, processing numerous thoughts at a rapid speed, and I get so exhausted that by the time they leave my mouth, I feel so sorry for anyone on the opposite end of those thoughts, listening. It is a battle I have to fight every day, especially when there are a number of circumstances happening at once that are making me anxious while trying to decipher them.

So to everyone who can relate, I see you. But for that person who is reading this, thinking, "This girl sounds like a complete weirdo!" Let me just reassure you that I am one, and I'd rather own every part of me than look down on myself ungraciously and be judgmental. I've already spent far too many years of my life doing that, so I won't.

And before you think I subscribe to the notion of "this is just me; take it or leave it," I want to let you know that while I am all for growth and evolving as a human being, I've learned that how you navigate these parts of yourself makes all the difference. God's Word tells us two key truths concerning this matter:

1. "Life and death are in the power of the tongue" (Proverbs 18:21, BSB).

2. "For as he thinketh in his heart, so is he" (Proverbs 23:7, KJV).

Knowing this helped me change the way I spoke and thought about myself. I'm naturally extremely hard on myself, and I had to learn to be softer with myself. I had an aha moment when thinking what I needed in my relationships, whether platonic or romantic, was that in knowing my personality, you'd know to be soft with me. Maybe I needed this because I was so hard on myself that I was trying to externally create a soft place for me to land. I craved that so much in life, that feeling of knowing I had a soft safety net just waiting there to catch me when life would knock me down or, worse, when I'd be the one knocking myself down.

Fear can be an extremely crippling device of the enemy, and if we allow this lie to take over our minds and emotions, it can and will prevent us from walking into the beautiful purpose God has planned for our life. Listen to the word of God. "For God hath not given us the spirit of fear; but of power, and of love, and of a sound mind" (2 Timothy 1:7, KJV).

> "Peace I leave with you; my peace I give you. I do not give to you as the world gives. Do not let your hearts be troubled and do not be afraid" (John 14:27, NIV).

> "Have I not commanded you? Be strong and courageous. Do not be afraid; do not be discouraged, for the Lord your God will be with you wherever you go" (Joshua 1:9, NIV).

I often reflect on that night Jesus came into my Bronx apartment and swooped me up like the knight in shining armor he is, reminding and reintroducing me to his love, his character, my best friend. When you're loved like that, you think, "This is it! I mean, what more can I possibly need?" While this is true, I've come to learn there are so many glorious layers.

The Word tells us He takes us from glory to glory, and I am experiencing it as I share. The past couple of weeks have been an emotional roller coaster during a propelling breakthrough as I come through this season, and *my mind is blown away.* In a nutshell, this season has been one of waiting, patiently waiting. As I've been waiting, I have earnestly prayed, praised God in advance, cried, been frustrated, and been overwhelmed, trying to figure out what God wants me to do while waiting.

It has been three years since that night and season, and I am just now realizing what I had been missing all along, and I praise God for his grace, his mercy, and his love. See, the past couple of weeks, I've been in this cloud, and I really wish I had a better explanation, but it is almost like my mind isn't my mind. I realize, as I'm telling you my experience in real time, how crazy it sounds, but I pray it's still reaching you.

God was teaching me more patience and to trust him always in all the ways! The realization of not knowing myself began a great work. I had a burning to desire to seek God more and more every day, every chance I had.

Who better to show me who I am than the One who created me? Knowing whose you are is really the game changer.

On this quest, here's what I've learned. The word of God lets us know our identity in Christ. So now that I know Christ, I know how to find myself, and that's what I began to experience. In this space of not knowing who I was, I began to feel things of the past that no longer fed my spirit fade away, and the scary part was that it started to include people.

In a dream/vision, God revealed a graduation to me where I sabotaged myself by intentionally missing my walk. I wanted to be there because I was rushing back to make it on time, but something was also holding me back, weighing me down. In the dream, I was encouraging every one of my peers but was OK missing my walk, although I wanted to make it there in time, so I began to reflect on what God revealed to me, and it blew my mind wide open to another stratosphere of growth and self-realization, God's realization.

I went from all these major life experiences back-to-back, throwing myself from one to the next. But when Jesus finds you, a spark ignites and sets your soul on fire! So here I was, thinking I'd spent the time having my intimate closet time with the Lord, my breakthrough divine therapy sessions. I'd repented; I'd poured and cried my soul out, releasing all the feelings and traumas that were holding me back.

The peace that I experienced once I released everything at the feet of Jesus my King and my friend then I began to feel something I'd have never felt, so I thought I had everything I now needed. So I began praying, trusting, fasting, waiting for my miracle and began to bask in the constant peace that surpasses all understanding.

Another one of my favorite traits of God is just when you think you have it figured out, He reveals another layer as if it's to remind you He is the *only* One who knows, period.

As I began to see what God was revealing to me, I then realized I was an extrovert living as an introvert. I was fearless but had been living fearfully. I was expressive but had been remaining silent when I should be speaking up. So there I was; I had created this little world within myself, living as a shell of myself.

Now as difficult as that self-realization is, once you get there, there's no turning back, baby! Once your spirit has revealed what your soul needs to align, it's either be still or go forward, but backward just isn't an option. It is truly a renewing transformation, a metamorphosis preparing you for takeoff, flying like an eagle, knowing that the work that Christ has begun in you He will complete until He returns.

Glory be to God!

Love Letters to the Lover of My Soul

Dear God,

This is my first time writing my prayers out to you, and I like it. I love it actually.

It's amazing when we write words, I still hear the words without speaking a word aloud. So though I know you know my thoughts, I know you hear my words and now read my words.

How beautiful! How beautiful are *you*! This journey with you has been a blessing because you are *the blessing and the blesser*! Wow. Thank you for never leaving me or forsaking me, even when I don't deserve it. You fight for me, even when I don't deserve it. You love me, even when I don't deserve it. I am blessed by you. What a *mighty God*!

***

Dear God,

Help me. You tell us that in all things you work for the good of those who love you and have been called according to your purpose. God, be with me. As you know, I recently left my job, and I'm nervous of what this might do to my relationship. He is not happy about me quitting my job, and I know it's placing a lot of weight on his shoulders, and I don't want that for him, Father. I know you're working on us both in this season, and I want to just say thank you in advance. There is never a time you have not provided for me and sustained me in every season. I will *not* doubt you. I will not fear the unknown. I am simply uncertain, and that is OK. For you let us know, "Faith is confidence in what we hope for and assurance about what we do not see." So, Father, keep me focused on the vision, but most importantly keep me focused on you. So through my faith, I will not only make my vision a reality through your grace but also bring others closer to you through it. Thank you for loving me. Thank you for discernment. Thank you for allowing me to take a leap of faith into *your* arms, dear God. Thank you in advance.

***

I see now I've been suppressing so much of myself because I feel like, being a mother of two children, I should have it all together. I am extremely hard on myself, and I resent myself for it. I didn't even know that it was possible to resent yourself, but I do. Cover me, Father. I need to feel you, hear you, please. I need you, and thank you for being with me. In Jesus' mighty name, I pray. Amen.

***

Dear God,

I thank you for loving me and accepting me with all my flaws. I love seeing the way you work and all the signs and wonders that not only give me hope but make me excited about the new thing you have begun in me and around me.

As I began to peel back some layers one by one, I think I have some conclusions but You are my conclusion Lord. So wherever I need correction, I am willing and ready to receive it. I think that possibly through my past hurt I have allowed things people have spoken over me to land without assessing these things before I let them hold space in my mind. These are all people I love so sometimes I think because they "love" me their intentions are pure but something doesn't sit well in my spirit. So lead me Father. Give me eyes to see and ears to hear, thank you for my eyes to see and ears to hear. I know when I submit my ways to you Father, You will make my path straight. So I leave it at your feet. Make me bold to stand up against any adversary and Thank You for fighting battles I know nothing of and for the ones I have been testament to. Thank You. In Jesus name Amen

***

Dear God,

Thank you. I have so much to say, but I can sum it up with a huge thank-you.

Thank you for your grace. Thank you for your mercy. Thank you for loving me.

***

Dear God,

I know what you mean when you tell us to put on the full armor, but it gets hard. Now don't get me wrong. I know greater is he in me than the emotional turmoil during my trials, but it gets difficult at times. I thank you so much for my support system, most of all the Holy Spirit, who is an amazing friend to me, always has been, and just consistent. Thank you for blessing me with someone who listens to me and leads me to you always.

This season has been particularly difficult with managing my emotions, and while writing this, I'm realizing maybe that is my lesson in this season, "how to manage my emotions." So I'm going to plan to do that now.

So I thank you for wisdom. Thank you for the Holy Spirit. Thank you for Jesus Christ. Thank you for me loving me. I *love* you.

***

Dear God,

Thank you for being amazing. I continue to see you working for me, through me, and around me, and I praise *your* name forever for it and so much more. In Jesus's precious, *almighty name, amen*!

***

Dear God,

I've reached this new chapter, this new awakening of hope, self-discipline, self-control, consistency, and faith. You continue to teach me so much, and I am grateful for the lessons and renewing of my mind.

***

Dear God,

Being a stay-at-home mom is a blessing and also difficult for me. I am so beyond grateful to have this precious time with my children, but at times it can get heavy with emotions.

***

Dear heavenly Father,

I am so grateful to you for all my blessings. My family is in a safe, warm, and comfortable home. You make sure we have food. We lack nothing. I lack nothing. You always provide me with everything I need, and I praise you for it!

Father, I come to you because I need a miracle, a financial breakthrough. Though things are not where I want them to be financially, I know you have already made a way, and I trust and believe you for it. I thank you for the peace that surpasses all understanding. I ask for wisdom to be ready and prepared to handle what you have in store. I also thank you for the wisdom given. I can clearly identify the areas you are improving and revealing.

***

Dear Father,

Thank *you*! The more I learn, the more I love you. The more I learn, the more I see how much you love me. I'm battling feelings of not doing enough and doing too much. At times I feel my personality is so complex that only *you* can understand me, and since *you* created me, I don't know if you're being biased. Ha ha! I joke, but I'm kind of serious.

Please help me stop being so hard on myself. Please help me stop overthinking because I trust you always in all ways. There's no question or doubt there, but my mind can't seem to stop. I only want to please *you*, but sometimes I find that I feel the need to please people, and I know you want us to love and support each other, but sometimes I need to say no, and it can be difficult. Jesus was always so strong in all situations, of a sound mind in all situations, and with Jesus as my *King*, I can look to *him* for guidance. Thank God. Amen!

***

Dear Father,

You are blowing my mind and expanding my heart and my faith. I can't thank you enough for loving me.

***

Dear heavenly Father,

Thank you. You always amaze me with your grace. Every time I think I understand just how much you love me, you reveal more of your love for me and teach me more of who you created me to be, which makes me love me, and I am so grateful! Thank you for being my loving Father, my Provider. You have secured my soul through my King, Jesus Christ, who have shown me the way to you. Thank you for the Holy Spirit, who has led me to the way. I will praise you all the days of my life!

***

I saw a rainbow on a Sabbath morning; it was so beautiful that I went to get my phone to capture the rainbow. By the time I got back, it was gone, as if God was showing me there are things that are just between us.

That same God wants a relationship with you, a personal relationship with you. He loves you more than any love you've ever known. I love him.

All praise to the Most High, my heavenly Father. Amen.

Milton Keynes UK
Ingram Content Group UK Ltd.
UKHW012153091123
432302UK00003B/21

9 798822 921214